AT THE EDGE OF THE SEA

SHAY MACKAY

Tehom Center Publishing is a 501(c)3 nonprofit publishing feminist and queer authors, with a commitment to elevate BIPOC writers. Its face and voice is Rev. Dr. Angela Yarber.

Paperback ISBN: 978-1-966655-20-6

Ebook ISBN: 978-1-966655-21-3

CONTENTS

For Diana,
thank you for helping me find the magic in every day.

This collection of essays and poems has been years in the making, with some pieces written during visits to the ocean, retreats in the woods, or for specific newsletter articles and sermons. Part of my call, as a spiritual leader and as a human being, is to discover and celebrate the Holy all around and within me - and encourage others to do the same.

I have titled it *At the Edge of the Sea*, speaking to the new and unexpected things that can wash up at our feet on the incoming tide like beach glass, tumbled, thrown, washed clean and reshaped into something different.

And so, too, can life toss us around, chipping, cracking, polishing. Within that tumult, and the periods of calm between waves, is where we find the sacred, both in ourselves and in the world around us.

Mysticism

I've always been a bit of a mystic, as you'll see in the essay "The Prairie Wind," and I've embraced it more as I matured. I've also become more intentional about it, and while I'll never fully understand what it means to live life mystically, I have, over time, clumsily found some language to put as much of a container around mysticism as I can - which isn't much, to be sure. Language and logic create structure with parameters and limitations, and that's really not what mysticism is about. Regardless, here's the best I can do:

Mysticism is an openness to experiencing the sacred everywhere and in everything. When we surrender to that possibility, the moments of recognition of this truth are so powerfully expansive that we can never forget them - even if they last only a few seconds.

Self-identified "queer mystic" Jan Phillips says, mysticism is "not the knowledge of something, but the experience of something…an experience of communion."

This is not to say that once you have a mystical experience you are always living in an enlightened way of being. For most of us, mystical moments are brief and rare, and then real life crashes back in on us – or we crash back into it. Many of us spend the time in between these experiences trying to recreate them, trying to find that portal again, trying to find our way back to the ultimate connectedness of love and light.

For some people, this search looks like meditation in any of its variants: an effort to focus and empty themselves, to open themselves to receive, or to surrender themselves to become.

For others, the desire to connect deeply with something larger than themselves in a transformative way leads into action, and a belief that only through compassion, empathy, and generosity will we be welcomed into communion with the divine.

For some it is prayer, for others it's nature; some seek it in relationships and others in artistic creativity.

Some of us try all of the above, but most of us don't try at all – not even aware of the possibility of something deeper and more profound than our daily life's status quo.

Here's the deal: when a mystical experience happens it catches us completely off-guard, hopefully in a good way, but not always, and shakes us to our core, and then we go on living our lives, different but the same, maybe talking about "that one time…" or keeping it as a sacred secret we pull out and look at only when we are alone. We simply go on being, with just a little bit more space in our soul.

Process Thinking (or Process Theology)

I've come to believe that our everyday journeys through life are (whether we know it or not, whether we admit it or not) spiritual journeys, and spiritual journeys are pilgrimages. As a mystic, I am always looking for the Holy, everywhere, and this led me to process theology.

Deeper thinkers than I have written many, many books about what process theology is, so I'm just going to borrow from them to give a brief introduction:

In an article on his website *Open Horizons*, Jay McDaniel says:

> Ultimately process thinking is an attitude and outlook on life, and a way of interacting with the world. It is not so much a rigidly defined worldview as it is a way of feeling the presence of the world and responding with creativity and compassion.

The universe is an ongoing process of development and change, never quite the same from moment to moment. Every entity in the universe is best understood as a process of becoming that emerges through its interactions with others. And this leads us to interconnectedness - the universe as a whole is a seamless web of interconnected events, none of which can be completely separated from the others. Everything is connected to everything else and contained within everything else.

In process theology, *everything* is a dynamic process, constant change and movement – the endless cycles within nature of birth and death, growth and decay; our constant growth as human beings, both individual and collective, in learning and understanding; and ultimately, for process theologians, that revelation is not just something of the past but is ongoing, in every moment in every thing.

The way of process thinking is both/and – embracing paradox, contradiction, and complexity. It allows us to celebrate beauty in the midst of destruction, to feel grief in the midst of joy, to begin to understand Love is the ultimate power of the universe even as terrible things happen. It does not make excuses, nor claim to understand the ways in which God (or whatever you call that great Mystery) moves within the world – it only affirms that God *is* moving within the world, along with us, *all the time.*

In his book *Process Theology: Embracing Adventure with God*, theologian Bruce G. Epperly says, "God moves within the circumstances from which our lives emerge, bringing forth possibilities for creative transformation."

And this, for me, is the core of process thought. *We are part of the process.*

Unlike tumbled, transformed beach glass the tide leaves at our feet, we have agency over our lives. Where can we guide the shaping? When do we surrender and when do we fight? How can we position ourselves to gaze further into the depths of the waters tossing us about and when is it best to reach for the sunlight sparkling on the surface?

This is, in the end, in the beginning, who we are (co-creators) and why we are here (to transform the interconnected *everything*).

As Epperly says, "God creates and also responds. Our actions can either enhance or diminish God's presence in the world, shaping the texture of God's activity in the world."

Defamiliarization

Many years ago, I was introduced to the concept of *ostranenie* - a literary term coined by Russian writer and critic Viktor Shklovsky in his 1917 essay "Art as Technique." It is an artistic technique used to defamiliarize what is known so that we can know it more deeply. As writer Anaïs Nin explained in *The Novel of the Future*, "It is the function of art to renew our perception. What we are familiar with we cease to see. The writer shakes up the familiar scene, and as if by magic, we see a new meaning in it."

I like to play with this concept in my writing, to take something as banal as standing in the check-out line at Target and turn it into a meaningful moment. We live in a world in motion, each moment full of both the holy and the mundane. Where are the places during the journeys of our everyday lives that contain an invitation to connect with something profound?

This intentional practice of noticing the sacred is what makes us mystics; and to be able to notice something we've seen a hundred times but never really *seen* before, we must learn to see differently.

Let's start at the edge of the sea, watching the tides come in and go out, leaving treasures and talismans in the sand at our feet. We can interact with these things – the bits and pieces of flotsam, the waves themselves, what's partially buried in the sand, and what's floating in the tide pools.

By interacting we become part of the process — and in that process we will, hopefully, find what we never even knew we were looking for.

The Parts of This Book

There are four parts to this book, each corresponding to an aspect of the mystical journey.

- Section I guides you through ways of preparing yourself to begin experiencing the world differently.
- Section II grounds you in a foundation of values, experiences, and decisions, all while reawakening wonder and reverence within you.
- Section III establishes the practices that enable you to move forward on this journey, a cyclical spiral of action and contemplation that serves to both fortify and inspire you.
- Section IV reminds you that you are but one drop in this ocean of life and the reality and responsibility of this journey is this: it is never just about you alone.

At the Edge of the Sea

Here, at the edge of the sea
I see a world in constant motion,
a flowing rhythm
of sounds, smells, sights;
in and out,
bringing water,
wonder,
waste,
from beyond the boundaries
of what I know,
from the edge
of the ends
of the earth.

Landing here at my feet –
bright, sharp, dead
and alive,
given and reclaimed without warning,
glimpsed, and then gone;
carried,
ferried by the tides
to other eyes,
moving to and from
a horizon barely seen
hardly understood
feared and found everywhere:

in our hearts
in our dreams
in the bright eyes of love
and those gone dim with age.

Horizons, urging us –
Come, here lies hope,
just a stone's throw away;
the next best thing to be laid
at your feet is here,
just beyond the edge
of safe and sound.

Come, let yourself be carried –
there is a new world to be found!

I. PREPARATION

PRESENCE AND OPENNESS

In order to arrive there,
To arrive where you are, to get from where you are not,
You must go by a way wherein there is no ecstasy.
In order to arrive at what you do not know
You must go by a way which is the way of ignorance.
In order to possess what you do not possess
You must go by the way of dispossession.
In order to arrive at what you are not
You must go through the way in which you are not.
And what you do not know is the only thing you know
And what you own is what you do not own
And where you are is where you are not.

— T.S. ELIOT, FROM "EAST COKER SECTION III," FOUR
QUARTETS

INVITATION

Be here now.

Here.
In this space;
this time and place.

Breathe in
and be here.

Breathe out
and plant your feet
in the solid strength
of this holy ground.

Feel it hold you.
Feel it mold
your body
into something sacred.

Feel Spirit
move through you,
move through all things,
collecting and connecting
moments in time.
Let Spirit awaken in you
that which connects you to All.

Center yourself in this moment.

Center yourself in this sacred moment
in your sacred body.

Open your holy heart
to the Holy everywhere,
to the Spirit that moves through all things.

Let it move through you now;
feel yourself flow into the love
and abundance this creation offers you;
and let that which is holy and true
flow out of you,
into this beautiful, broken world.

Section Introduction

In order to undertake any journey it is best to prepare yourself.

First, it is imperative that your faith in an ever-changing, dynamic, complex universe-in-process is strong; small miracles and immense transformations are happening everywhere, all the time. The deeper your belief in this constant creational cycle, the easier it will be for you to witness it, experience it, collaborate with it. If your faith feels more tentative, that's okay! Hang onto the small moments of evidence and experience that you find, examine them, embrace them, and eventually you will collect enough of them to bolster your belief.

Next, create a vast spaciousness within yourself. Life is an adventure full of possibilities and the more openness you can nurture in your mind and heart, the richer your experiences will be. Cultivate curiosity in yourself!

Most importantly, this way of being in the world - of being *of* the world - requires presence; a centered and grounded awareness of the now. Find a spiritual practice that assists you in this - meditation, mindfulness, centering prayer, intentional breathing, etc. The paradoxical nature of mysticism is that it asks you to be both hugely spacious and intentionally focused in your awareness.

> Healthy mysticism praises acts of letting go, of being emptied, of getting in touch with the space inside and expanding this until it merges with the space outside. Space meeting space; empty pouring into empty.
>
> — MATTHEW FOX, *CREATION SPIRITUALITY: LIBERATING GIFTS FOR THE PEOPLES OF THE EARTH*

Let There Be a Dawn!

We can begin anything we do - start our day, eat a meal, or walk into a meeting - with the intention to be open, flexible, and kind. Then we can proceed with an inquisitive attitude.

— PEMA CHODRON, *THE PLACES THAT SCARE YOU*

The alarm goes off or some noise wakes you out of deep sleep. You jerk awake, heart racing, and desperately try to get your bearings. Where are you? What time is it? What's happening?

For a few seconds everything you know about the world, about yourself, about life – none of it matters. Your mind can't grasp onto anything familiar. Time has stopped. There is no "you" and "everything else." There's just EVERYTHING and NOTHING. Your heightened awareness takes everything in and yet nothing is familiar.

It's over almost before it's begun, and you begin making sense again out of what's happening around you. You respond appropriately: hit snooze, get up to soothe a crying child, close the window on the barking dog at the neighbor's house.

But for a moment you were experiencing life differently – to the very core of you. For a moment, when you were awakened, you were transported out of the familiar and into the unknown. It was scary, but also exhilarating! When was the last time your heart pounded like that? When was the last time adrenaline rushed through your body so powerfully?

When was the last time you felt so alive?

Morning is when I am awake and there is a dawn in me. To be awake is to be alive. We must learn to reawaken and keep ourselves awake, not by mechanical aids, but by an infinite expectation of the dawn, which does not forsake us in our soundest sleep. I know of no more encouraging fact than the unquestionable ability of man to elevate his life by a conscious endeavor. It is something to be able to paint a particular picture, or to carve a statue, and so to make a few objects beautiful; but it is far more glorious to carve and paint the very atmosphere and medium through which we look, which morally we can do. To affect the quality of the day, that is the highest of arts.

— HENRY DAVID THOREAU, *WALDEN*

Let there be a dawn in you! Throw off sleep and jump willingly into the unfamiliar and the unknown. Affect the quality of your days with wonder and awe through conscious endeavor. Carve and paint yourselves anew into a wakefulness that sees this world the way we dream it to be – a wakefulness that inspires you to work toward creating that world unfailingly.

The Nose Flute

A few years ago, my family and I were fortunate enough to visit the big island of Hawai'i. One day we were walking through the lush greenness of the trail to Waimea Falls and came upon a demonstration table. An older Hawaiian woman stood there, under an umbrella, with various items from traditional Hawaiian culture on the table in front of her. As we approached, she picked up the Hawaiian nose flute and began to play - holding the foot long piece of carved wood up to her nose and exhaling. Her fingers lay relaxed on the flute, moving gently to help shape the melody she played.

After a brief song she looked at me and asked, "Do you know why we play the flute with our noses?"

I shook my head - in fact, I had never even heard of such a thing!

She said, "Our mouths talk. Out of them come all sorts of meanness and nasties, sometimes without even thinking, and then they can't be taken back. They settle in the heart, hurting, an open wound, forever out there, hurting." And with those words she touched a fist to her chest, clenched tight and hard against her body.

"But," she continued, "with the pureness of our breath, we can soothe and heal. We can create beauty and put it out into the world."

Her hand relaxed and lay upon her chest open and whole.

I wondered, "Can you play and sing at the same time?"

With a great laugh she said, "I"ll try!"

And she did! She played and chanted all at once, clumsily, beautifully, as we all looked on in wonder.

Then she smiled brilliantly and said, "Anything is possible!"

She took my hand, holding it firmly in her older ones, looked me in the eye and put a small woven frond square onto my palm. It fit perfectly.

"This is a possibility ball. To remind you anything is possible!"

I thought of the argument I had had that morning.

I thought of the possibility of letting go of words, inadequate and troublesome, the possibility of breathing out - pure and true - apology, compassion, understanding, forgiveness.

I thought of the possibility of breathing in - deeply - peace, light, connection... and breathing out a song of love.

RADICAL WELCOME

Henri Nouwen claims that true hospitality can only be offered by those who "have found the center of their lives in their own hearts." This means that the very first step in creating a space of inclusion and transformation is to go within. Each aspect of ourselves is important, has something to teach us, and combines to create the whole of who we are. As the Sufi poet Rumi writes in "The Guest House," we must welcome in each feeling, each piece of ourselves because "each has been sent/as a guide from beyond."

It is this embracing of the stranger, of the unknown, of the mystery that makes true hospitality a radical act. We must paradoxically choose to intentionally create the conditions for reverence and greater life, while also choosing to surrender control of how the story will unfold. As we work within to integrate all aspects of ourselves, we are invited to rest in the movement of something larger, something deeper.

This is true not only within our own souls or among the walls and boundaries of our safe and known spaces, but extends beyond, out into the world, into the interconnected web of all creation. We must move beyond acting as if we are guests here on Earth, entitled and devoid of responsibility. We must move beyond ideas of dominion and control, choosing instead to participate in acts of co-creation toward healing and greater life.

This means, also, moving beyond comfort and ease, entering fully into the suffering of our world and all Her inhabitants. As Abraham ran out into the desert seeking and embracing strangers, radical hospitality calls us to seek out that which is unfamiliar and uncomfortable; as Nouwen says, "we are called to reach out with courageous honesty" into the places and moments that break us open. It is within these moments, when we allow ourselves to be vulnerable with strangers and with mystery, that we can deeply experience the holy and move beyond ourselves into the place where spirit flows freely.

CENTER AND OPEN

When I was in college, I took a pottery class. I learned how to get my hands dirty, wedging the clay with the force of my body until it was ready to be put on the wheel. This was a process of pushing and rolling the clay, forcing all the air out of it while blending all of its particles into a consistency perfect for pottery.

The next step was to center the clay on the wheel, a critical step as it is the foundation of the pot - and the pot is only as balanced and strong as the centering. I learned how to center that clay, and myself, as the wheel spun and then finally, how to open it, pushing my thumbs into the center and slowly pulling upwards and outwards until a plate or bowl began to form.

> The life of a human is a self-evolving circle, which, from a ring imperceptibly small, rushes on all sides outwards to new and larger circles, and that without end...the heart refuses to be imprisoned... it tends outward with a vast force, to immense and innumerable expansions.
>
> — RALPH WALDO EMERSON, "CIRCLES"

It is in our nature, it is in our hearts to expand outwards, to emerge into the world with the vast force of our convictions and our compassion. The spiritual journey calls us to contemplation and personal growth, to seek our own individualized truth, to be centered in ourselves and our beliefs – *and* it calls us to action, to seeing and being in the world differently, to opening our minds and our hearts.

If you aren't both centering and opening your clay at the right rate, you create an uneven rim that will pull the whole thing out of line. The practice of hands working material rewires the body, and the body and the brain learn to listen to something besides themselves. They learn to be responsive to reality.

— AMY WELDON, "THE SPINNING SELF"

The practice of centering rewires us, helps us learn to listen to our core convictions and values. It helps us open to the reality of the world we are a part of. It helps us open to being more a part of the world.

II. FOUNDATION

MEMORY AND WONDER

When you as a child learned to speak,
It's not that you didn't know words—
It's that, from the centuries, you knew so many,
And it's hard to choose the words that will be your own.
From those centuries we human beings bring with us
The simple solutions and songs,
The river bridges and star charts and song harmonies
All in service to a simple idea:
That we can make a house called tomorrow.
What we bring, finally, into the new day, every day,
Is ourselves. And that's all we need
To start. That's everything we require to keep going.
Look back only for as long as you must,
Then go forward into the history you will make.
Be good, then better. Write books. Cure disease.
Make us proud. Make yourself proud.
And those who came before you?
When you hear thunder,
Hear it as their applause.

— ALBERT RÍOS, FROM "A HOUSE CALLED
TOMORROW"

INVITATION

Listen, this is important.
Go deep.
Deeper still.

Go deep inside to the well within your soul,
the pool that holds the memory
of the story of all that came before,
and more.
The story of all creation.

The memory of the story of your creation.
Go deep.

To the words written on your heart that speak of the now,
that speak of the who of You,
the words that sing of all you love, and those that weep.
Go deep.

Deep into the tissues and muscles and bones
of your arms and legs and hips and neck, your hands and feet,
the soft and strong parts of you that shift and move,
re-arranging and re-interpreting
where you've been and where you're going.
Go deep.

Go deep and find that which is fully, wholly, beautifully You.

Section Introduction

As you journey through life, it is often helpful to remember your history and find your foundation. Rediscover the values and experiences that have shaped you - and then get rid of the ones that no longer serve you.

Most importantly, reclaim childlike awe and wonder, let life in and treat it with both reverence and uncoordinated glee - be a little rough with it, turning it over in your hands, holding it up to your nose and taking a deep whiff, bending your ear and listening for the song of the ocean or the marching of ants. Use all of your senses to experience the world of which you are a part.

We are, always, both where we've been and where we're going. The only control we have over either of those things is what we do with them *right now*.

> To survive,
> Let the past
> Teach you--
> Past customs,
> Struggles,
> Let
> These
> Help you.
> Let them inspire you,
> Warn you,
> Give you strength.
> But beware:
> God is Change.
> Past is past.
> What was
> Cannot
> Come again.

To survive,
know the past.
Let it touch you.
Then let
The past
Go.

— OCTAVIA E. BUTLER, PARABLE OF THE TALENTS

Dance of the Prairie Wind

My first word for God was Wind.

I grew up literally as far from an ocean as it is possible to be on this continent. My childhood home was 100 miles from the geographic center of North America.

All I knew of salt water was what I read about in books, saw in movies, and tasted in my own tears.

But I knew waves. I knew what it was to watch ebbs and flows caused by mysterious, unknown forces, to watch as surfaces shimmered at the apex, catching light and carrying it down with them into the depths.

I knew natural rhythms, movement that can soothe or agitate, pound against your body or caress as softly as a whisper.

I knew of horizons, vistas, wide open spaces and unending views. I knew what it was to never lose sight of the sun as it moved across an endless sky from sunrise to sunset.

There aren't a lot of trees among the great plains, either, but I knew the sounds of rustling plants and secret, scurrying critters, the rise and fall of insect sounds and bird songs.

And I knew what it was to stand in the middle of a vast, open field of prairie grass and feel God's touch brush against me as the prairie wind danced across the plains.

ROAD TRIP

My parents were both school teachers, so as I was growing up not only did my sister and I have summer vacation, but the whole family was free. We loved road trips – and before there were all the rules about...um...safety, my dad would pack us into our little blue Chevette hatchback and off we would go on some adventure. From our starting place smack dab in the middle of North Dakota, over time we explored in all directions – South Dakota, Manitoba, Montana, and Minnesota; and while Mount Rushmore and the Badlands and all of the 10,000 lakes were beautiful and awe-inspiring, the scenic destinations were not my favorite parts of these trips.

We would pack the car the night before our journey began so that we could leave immediately upon waking the next morning. My sister and I would then desperately try to sleep, telling each other that the sooner we fell asleep the sooner morning would come, but anticipation always kept us revved up until way past bedtime. Just a few hours later, well before dawn, Dad would rouse us and bundle our half-sleeping bodies into the car – pajamas, pillows, blankets, and all. The backseat was full of luggage and coolers, leaving the hatch available for my sister and I to lie in. It was a soft, warm nest and we would doze there while my parents finished packing up.

And then we would drive.

Dad was the driver – it was one of his favorite things to do; mom was the navigator (who fell asleep the minute the car was in motion); and my sister and I – we were the watchers, the dreamers, the wonderers. We drove in silence, those first hours of pre-dawn darkness. If I lifted my head to peer over the backseat, I could see my dad's face in the rearview mirror, partially illuminated by the dashboard lights. If I held my breath and listened intently, I could hear my mother's deep, even breathing as she slept. I would raise my hands and press them against the window and feel the coolness of the morning, in direct contrast to the warmth of my sister's body curled up next to me.

And for an hour or two, I would lie on my back in the quiet, letting the motion of the car gently hypnotize me. I would gaze up through the hatchback window, counting stars as the city lights faded, making wishes on meteors streaking through the heavens; and I would lose myself in the slow and brilliant arrival of dawn.

Memorial Day

I grew up in the middle of North Dakota – part of a large extended German Catholic family, most of whom lived in tiny farming communities in the prairies around the central Missouri valley. Every year on Memorial Day, my dad's seven siblings, their spouses and all thirty-two of my cousins would pile into cars and head out – caravan style – for a long day of remembrance.

The first stop was the furthest away. We would start there and slowly make our way back home. It was the original family home-stead, a sprawling dairy and wheat farm in the middle of nowhere, settled and claimed by my grandfather just before World War II. It remains in the family still, although most of the land has been sold or rented out to larger food producers.

We would walk around, tour the old house my dad and his siblings grew up in, check out the milking barn, chase the chickens in the yard, hear stories of our parents' youth and life on the farm. And then we would pile back into the cars and parade down the dirt road to the tiny country Catholic church that served the commu-nity for far longer than any organized town existed. The church in which my grandmother and her sister came to marry two brothers, men they had never met before that day.

There's a small cemetery in this church's yard and it was the real reason we were all out there on those beautiful late May days. All fifty of us would wind our way through the tall grasses and tomb-stones, the adults pointing out those that we should pay attention to. Plastic flowers were placed, stones were cleaned, weeds were pulled – and stories were told.

This continued throughout the day as we stopped in each small town cemetery that held some beloved relative or friend. We would linger in one and have a picnic lunch, move quickly through another to avoid a surprise thunderstorm. One year we even had to find shelter in which to wait while a tornado passed by. And still the stories continued.

This may seem like a macabre way to spend time together on a precious holiday weekend, but it was so much more than just a bunch of people looking at graves and hanging onto the past. It was a re-weaving of the fabric of our family – a fabric that held us and healed us. Through the telling of the stories of where we came from, we remembered those who had started the weaving of that cloth, acknowledged their part in what we now were, and through the shared experience of remembering together my parents and aunts and uncles were ensuring that their children would under- stand the importance of the family community and teaching us how to continue weaving those threads long into the future.

I remember sitting in Catholic Mass, an adolescent looking around at those sitting in the pews with me, fascinated by their faces, by what I could read there in the unguarded moments of prayer and song.

What I saw moved my heart - I wanted to hear their stories. I wanted to listen - somehow I knew this would offer comfort. I also knew every single one of them deserved to be heard.

C.S. Lewis says "we are all possible gods and goddesses... there are no ordinary people."

There are no ordinary people.

Remember - Spirit moves through all things. This is the truth of who we are. Most of us have forgotten, or it has been buried under the effects of trauma or neglect, obscured by fear and grief. Most of us have lost our awareness of the divine within ourselves. We have lost our connection to the divine within others.

"Dear God, deliver me to my power to heal."

I remember being broken open by these words, written by Marianne Williamson. I remember thinking, "I want to be a healer." But I've learned that I cannot heal anyone. I can companion, witness, guide. I can offer words of encouragement for the journey, bolster faith when it is weak, provide gentle challenge when stories are stuck, offer guidance away from harmful thoughts. I can remind people of the fullness of their divinity and affirm their connection to all beings, and to God.

This is the story I've learned to tell about myself, and I've learned that the stories we tell about ourselves (to ourselves) matter. Our thoughts and words have power. And so, remember, our words have power, whether we are speaking them to ourselves, to others, or to Spirit. The power of prayer, the power of stories, the power of song, and the power of silence - the silence in which old words can settle and new ones can be found.

Be still and know that I am with you, that Spirit moves here among us, between us. Rest in my silent witness until you are ready to sing once more. I'll wait here with you as you close your eyes and listen, listen for the melody of the next verse of your song.

I'm here. I'm listening. Sing me your story.

———

I had a hard conversation last night; said some things I wish I hadn't to someone I love very much. Audre Lorde's daughter once told her that "if you keep your words all stopped up inside, one day they'll just explode out and punch you in the mouth."

There are people I love with whom certain topics are off the table. You probably have some of those, too. Politics, religion, white supremacy, climate change... It's a veritable smorgasbord stashed away in the hall closet, glimpsed when folding tables and chairs come out for a holiday family feast. The solitary light bulb hanging in the closet isn't even turned on, you just grab what you need to keep the peace and go, shutting the door quickly and tight.

Sometimes a brave (or clueless) soul will leave that closet door cracked, and harsh words creep out into the shadows, into the corners of the house, moving under the tables like a dog searching for crumbs, waiting, just waiting for a morsel to be dropped. And someone careless (or reckless) opens the moment with a casual comment - not a gauntlet thrown but a wink and a smirk. (Metaphorical of course, the only one actually smirking is the trickster who left the closet door open.)

And if you, or someone you love very much, is tired or stressed or hurting or scared, those harsh words pounce, exploding out like a punch in the mouth. And the dinner is lost. Chalk another ruined reunion up to politics, religion, white supremacy, climate change...

Last night years worth of holding it in came spewing out. No more agreeing to disagree - this was a fight to the death. Well, at least to sobs and shouts. And then, of course, no sleep, more tears, maybe some warm milk. And in the morning, half delirious and dehydrated, you manage to talk those shadows off the ledge and you think, "There's gotta be a better way to do this."

And maybe, for a moment, a day, a year, you find it - compassion, empathy, compromise - and you make your way back to relationship.

But sometimes those shadows, they're just always gonna be there. That's just how it is. So when you're tired or stressed or hurting or scared, all the words you've managed not to say are gonna come out. I'm hoping that each time they do they get weaker, you get stronger, and apology and forgiveness get easier.

I'm not saying that you should give up on your principles, or compromise your beliefs. Maybe just that we all could learn some more compassionate communication skills rather than live with dark closets and occasional punches in the mouth. I know that I, for one, have a long way to go, but each time I try I am able to shed a little more light on those hungry, angry, shadowy things.

And in the light, I can see them for what they are (careless, reckless) - and let them go.

Go on. Shoo! No crumbs here.

III. PRACTICE

CONTEMPLATION AND ACTION

You have to hear the sound before you play the sound.
It is you who have to hear it is you who have to hear it
is you who have to sit under the singing
of the bird it is you who have to sit in the
court of the bird to hear to assent to the
singing as in prayer being heard it is you who
have to sit in the court to assent
it is you who have to sit in a kind of silence.
The sound is there to turn inside out: what is
inside is not the bird not the bird but his presence.
You have to hear the sound before you play before
there is room to clap you have to hear the sound before
you dance as a candle as a candle-flame as
a flame on the waves with your hair flowed back.
The sound is there to turn inside out: what is
inside is not the bird not the bird but his presence.

— *JOHN TAGGART, FROM "INSIDE OUT" IS MUSIC*

INVITATION

Slow down.
Take your time.
Be still.

Everything around you is moving fast -
you don't have to.

You are the stone,
sun-kissed and caressed
by softly sifting Spirit.

You are the leaf,
floating,
cradled gently by cool, clear water.

And now, you are the rushing river of life
and the strength of its current
causing movement,
catching sunlight.

Do not be frenzied,
flow.

Flow
with a quiet strength,
a gentle intention,
a calm attention.

Flow,
and find that which you seek.

Section Introduction

The spiritual journey is a never-ending pilgrimage—a continuous cycle of departure, arrival, and return. It isn't something to be mastered; rather, it is something to be lived.

If the spiritual journey is something to be lived, then spiritual practice can help bring us back to our intention. Spiritual practice calls us to return and remember—to return to our intention, reflect on where we've been, and remember the journey we are on.

It is practice that allows us to wade a little further into the water each time we try, that enables us to go a little deeper each time we dive. And eventually we learn that we don't have to wait for the tide to bring experiences to us and lay them at our feet. We can move forward, find the tide, meet it, and become a part of the picking up, washing clean, noticing beauty, and celebrating it.

In 2021, in his article, "This Moment is Perfect," that appeared in *Lion's Roar Magazine*, Buddhist monk and teacher Thich Nhat Hanh wrote that "spiritual practice is not just sitting and meditating. Practice is looking, thinking, touching, drinking, eating, and talking. Every act, every breath, and every step can be practice and can help us to become more ourselves."

Here are a few spiritual practices to try:

- Slow down. (It's that simple!)
- Interact with everything and everyone as if it was holy. (Because it is!)
- See if you can find a balance between contemplation and action that works for you. Perhaps you need more of one than the other. At certain times you may be incapable of one, and that's okay - focus on the other, but don't forget about the first. We can only continue on this path by doing both.

Target Practice

I've been thinking a lot lately about patience; more specifically, about how I could use more of it in my life. A couple of weeks ago, I was standing in the check-out line at Target, grumbling to myself about picking the "wrong" line. You know, the line that's not moving at all while those on either side appear to be zipping by; the line where the shoppers ahead of you have a handful of expired coupons to use, can't find their checkbook, or picked a damaged item and are now waiting for a replacement to be found.

Well, on this day, the line I had chosen wasn't moving because (in my opinion) the cashier was slow and distracted by chatting with her customers. As I impatiently shifted from foot to foot and sighed loudly while pretending to peruse the magazine covers in the rack, I eavesdropped on the conversation happening between the cashier and the customer in front of me. The cashier asked the woman about the cat litter box she was buying and I frowned and gave another sigh, anticipating an even longer wait.

And then I watched as the customer's head came up, her posture straightened, and her whole face lit up with a smile. She began talking about her daughter, whose cat was going to be the recipient of the many items she was buying. She told an amusing anecdote of the rambunctious cat and I found myself smiling as I was drawn into her story. The cashier laughed and nodded, maintaining eye contact and a gentle attentiveness as she continued to slowly slide items across the scanner and bag them.

When the story came to an end we were all laughing together and as the woman paid for her items and said goodbye, I realized the tension had left my body and the tight, frustrated knot that had lodged in my chest was gone. I had a smile on my face and I felt a million times better because of it; because a "slow" cashier had taken the time to ask a question, to really see the person in front of her; because sometimes while we are waiting a moment of grace occurs.

Maybe it's not always important to be done the fastest or get there the quickest. Maybe sometimes it's better to stop and breathe, smell the roses. Maybe sometimes we need to take the circuitous route rather than go in a straight line.

And maybe, someday, I'll be the person who can make someone's face light up when I take the time to ask about her daughter's cat.

The Hammock

My partner and I got a two-person hammock. Not one of those curl-up-around-you-cocoon-hammocks, but one with the spreader bar, so that two can lay comfortably side by side. We set it up in the backyard, in semi-rural New Hampshire where there is very little light pollution, and we laid in it for hours, star-gazing, sometimes talking quietly, but mostly in silence. It was a much-needed respite from the busy-ness of our lives, and an invaluable gift of time with and for each other, for ourselves, for the beauty all around us.

For just a few hours on that autumn evening, Diana and I stopped rushing, stopped getting ahead of ourselves. Instead, we got still and quiet. We became present, to the moment and to each other.

The universe, the billions of galaxies of stars over our heads, welcomed us in, their million-year-old light serving to balance the heady rush of time that pushes us through each day. The light of countless stars, countless eons old, and the anxiety of countless outcomes of countless futures canceled each other out – and there, swaying in our hammock, holding hands, we fell into a moment of peace.

Now, I don't know if you've ever been in a hammock, but it is not usually a graceful experience. Getting into and out of the thing can be treacherous. Add another body into the mix and you've got plenty of fodder for America's Funniest Home Videos. It is a delicate balancing act of shifting weight and body parts, making sure your feet, and not your head, are aimed for the ground. I'm pretty sure the first time I got out of the two-person hammock Diana nearly flew off the other side as I put my feet on the ground and let the thing swing. But after a few tries we figured it out, and actually became quite good at achieving the right balance in order to lay comfortably and swing gently, to breathe deeply and connect.

To Whom Shall We Pray?

I was speaking once with a middle-aged couple – acquaintances of mine I had run into while out doing errands. The woman had just been released from the hospital and was telling me all about her frightening health scare. Her husband listened quietly, but I could tell he was shaken up by what had happened. The woman asked me to say a prayer with them – for her health, but more importantly, she said, for her husband who was so scared and worried for her. I looked at him, met his eyes, and asked him where he finds comfort, wondering to whom or what we should pray.

He thought for many moments, considering my question quietly. Finally, he said, "The trees are where I find comfort. I look at them and see how beautiful and strong they are and I wonder, How have they survived? I ask them, How are you still standing after all you've been through?"

And then he said, "But I know how they survive, Shay. I watch them in the storm, when the wind is blowing, and they bend, you know? They bend in the wind and they survive."

And it was in that moment that he recognized there was something in the trees that was also inside him. In the moment he took to think about it, to watch and listen, the trees told him their stories of resiliency and steadfastness - and in so doing, helped him see the same beauty and strength within himself.

And I could literally see the change in him as he stood up straighter, made more direct eye contact, reached out to grab his wife's hand and tell her how wonderful it had been to hear her voice again after her surgery. I saw, in those few minutes, the courage and resiliency inside him blossom after he was able to open his eyes to seeing those things in the world around him.

The Sing Along

I worked at a memory care and senior care facility for one year during my training to be a chaplain. I would often go to the common areas on each floor and play old hymns on the pianos there to entertain the residents and help calm staff.

On the second floor lived a woman named Harriet, a quite elderly woman with advanced dementia. Harriet, strapped into her wheelchair and left in the common room to enjoy the music, was almost constantly calling out in a loud and strident voice, "Help me, please! Oh please, help me!"

These were the only words I had ever heard her speak, and she yelled them no matter what the circumstances. Most of the staff had learned to ignore it, after checking that there really was nothing she needed. We took it as another symptom of her dementia.

One day I was playing piano for the residents and Harriet was there, calling out as usual. While I was playing (and trying to ignore her calls), I wondered what this scene would look like to a visitor - what would they think if they stepped off the elevator, into the common room, to see the staff and the chaplain ignoring an old woman's pleas for help?

My heart cracked open and I could no longer ignore Harriet, so I went over to her in case, perhaps, this time there was actually something wrong.

I knelt in front of her wheelchair and took her hands in mine. I asked, "What's wrong, Harriet?"

She answered, "Nothing is wrong."

After my initial surprise at her coherent answer, I smiled and nodded and then asked another question, "Why do you keep calling out for help?"

And she looked directly into my eyes, squeezed my hands, and said, "I'm not calling for help. I was just singing along to the beautiful music!"

One afternoon, while working at a homeless shelter, I was busy helping get lunch prepared when someone tapped me on the shoulder. I turned to find Andy, a regular guest, standing behind me, quietly crying and desperately trying to stay on his feet. Andy was extremely drunk and, by the looks of him, had been for several days. I took one look at him and said quietly, "Come with me."

I led him into our small chapel and sat down next to him, trying to figure out what to say, but before I could get a word out, Andy fell apart. In the dim light and deep stillness of that place, he wept as if his heart was breaking, and mine broke as I listened. We sat that way for a long time, close but not touching, through his tears and into the silence that followed.

Finally, Andy started talking. He told me how long he had been sober this time, what had happened to trigger this relapse, what he could remember of his behavior from the past few days, and how it all made him feel. He expressed remorse, disappointment, self-disgust, fear, anger and confusion – and deep, deep sorrow.

When Andy was done speaking I asked if there was anything I could do for him. He grabbed my hands.

"Say a prayer, Shay. Will you just pray with me?"

So I closed my eyes and prayed.

When I was done, I looked up to find Andy watching me. He said, through more tears, "Thank you. You're truly an angel, come down to earth." I blushed and smiled, shaking my head and muttering that I wasn't any such thing. He squeezed my hands, looked directly into my eyes and said, "Don't be embarrassed. You are an angel."

And then he leaned in even closer to me and whispered, "It's ok. I'm an angel, too."

Authority

It seems to me that when we talk about authority what we're really talking about is trust. And not an easy trust or a simple trust, but trust that is enigmatic and paradoxical. A trust in both a grasp of power and a submission to something bigger than ourselves. A trust in both pride and humility. A trust in both wisdom and ignorance.

Not only that, but authority also inherently creates "other"; there must be a source or agent of authority and a someone(s) receiving, responding, submitting, or serving. In a time when we are increasingly distrustful of binaries and dichotomies, authority becomes even harder to swallow.

And the sad truth is that so many of us have had our trust betrayed over and over again – broken promises, abuses of power, boldfaced lies, and subtle oppressions from religious leaders, politicians, teachers, parents, bosses, etc.

I'm sorry for all the scars we bear, both personally and communally. It's no wonder that the younger generations require their leaders to earn their authority rather than be followed dutifully because of age or status or money. It's no wonder that it can feel so hard to claim our own authority, to voice even our deepest convictions, for fear of joining the ranks of those who have over-used and abused such things.

And yet...

Charles de Gaulle once wrote, "Nothing builds authority up like silence." We are constantly being told by our leaders, our ministers, our prophets that the voice of liberal religion must be heard in today's world; that our message is not only important, but imperative as a counterpoint to voices of oppressive, abusive authority that seem to control our society.

Yes, authority can be scary. So much so that even claiming our own can be very difficult. But there are things in which we've learned we can trust. In fact, liberal religion has identified several sources of authority in which we can depend: direct experience of mystery, words and deeds of prophetic people that have come before us, wisdom from the world's religions, humanist and scientific teachings, and spiritual practices of the myriad of Earth-centered traditions that have existed for thousands of years.

We're also learning, at least I hope we are, that the wisest and most powerful authority is that of the Love that binds us together in beloved community. There's a delicate balance to be found between our individual experiences and convictions and our collective values and visions, but if we trust in the both/and of that tension our fear and hesitation will be replaced by humble audacity to speak and act toward a shared vision.

So, yes. In response to de Gaulle's claim that our silence allows unhealthy authority to gain power and control, we must speak loudly and often with our own authority. But I wonder, if we look at his words with different emphasis, if there's another message there for us. What if what he was really saying was that nothing strengthens our own inner authority so much as silence – taking the time to be quiet and let the still, small voice within speak?

Because in order to stand up and make our voices heard in this world, we need to know what it is we want to say.

IV. INTEGRATION

CONNECTION AND CREATION

What we call the beginning is often the end
And to make an end is to make a beginning.
The end is where we start from...

With the drawing of this Love
and the voice of this Calling
We shall not cease from exploration
And the end of all our exploring
Will be to arrive where we started
And know the place for the first time.

— T.S. ELIOT, FROM LITTLE GIDDING SECTION V,
FOUR QUARTETS

INVITATION

Woven,
the fragmented strands of our lives
transformed.
Take one thin thread of delight
and one of despair;
one fragrant bloom
and one crumbling husk –
all flourishing is mutual,
all wholeness dependent on
this weaving.

From the debris of destruction
wind the vines of life,
seeking balance,
a relationship of giving
and taking,
a meeting of hearts,
blending of spirits,
a braiding of lives lived and
made stronger
by this creation,
made more elastic,
stretching to reach
more of the sun
than could ever be reached alone.

Together we absorb
the shock of a shuddering world.
Together we encircle
that which feels most important.
Together we cultivate
the conditions for life -
woven threads of faith,
unity, hope, joy, and love –
binding us, holding us
guiding us on our journey.

Section Introduction

In her book *Divining the Body* Jan Phillips reminds us, "We forgot we were sparks from the same flame, waves of the same sea, that as much as the Divine is around us, the Divine is within us, experiencing itself through every sense in our bodies."

One of the beautiful results of experiencing the universe-in-process in a mystical way is a falling away of your sense of self, a dissolving of the "otherness" that separates you from everything else. Having defamiliarized the world around you, you begin to experience it in new ways, start to understand the interplay and influence of each moment.

Understanding this connection, you can now join in celebration, be part of creation, again and again, transforming this world into a better, beautiful whole.

> Each time his [Pierre Teilhard de Chardin] knowledge of the physical world expanded, he found it necessary to reshape his understanding of the transcendent and to adjust his spirituality to the shape of the universe that was being revealed to him. He discovered that 'truth...can be preserved only by being continually enlarged.
>
> — KATHLEEN DUFFY, *TEILHARD'S MYSTICISM: SEEING THE INNER FACE OF EVOLUTION*

CHANCE ENCOUNTER

It was late spring, the kind of morning that smells like life - the green and brown scents of trees and earth. The morning sunlight was clear as glass, with just a hint of the shimmer the afternoon heat would bring.

I came down the stairs of my apartment building, stepping off onto the concrete of the courtyard. Immediately something caught my eye - just to the side of the walkway was a young rabbit, having a bit of a snack.

We noticed each other at the same moment, eyes locking, and both of us froze. In the instant before it bolted into the bushes, it was as if I saw everything - everything - at once - the sky, the sun, the grass; I could literally see the air that surrounded me, my vision contracted, the edges grayed out, and became so focused and yet I felt as if I was seeing everything.

What I saw was the connection - not connections plural - but The. One. Connection. The Spirit that Moves Through Everything.

All of this, too much for my mind (my words) to comprehend, but my SOUL felt its Truth. All of this in mere seconds, looking into the eyes of a wild rabbit, and then...

It was gone so fast I almost missed its movement - I mean the rabbit.

I mean the vision.

Three seconds of a morning nearly thirty years ago, and my heart has never forgotten, my mind still tries to explain, my soul promises to find again.

YIN AND YANG

A few days ago, while walking, I found myself smiling at the antics of all the busy little squirrels rushing around. At first, I moved briskly, my pace matching their frenetic energy as I walked for exercise, not really caring that I interrupted their work and sent them running for their burrows. But after a while, I found myself slowing down, attempting to quiet my steps and appear non-threatening. Gradually my breathing slowed and deepened, my energy centered, my body loosened and my spirit expanded until I was moving in mindfulness. The scents of freshly mown grass and the previous night's rain; the bursts of color from lovingly tended gardens; the music of birds, barking dogs, distant children playing; all combined to envelop me, engaging my senses and soothing my soul.

Suddenly I stopped, startled out of my reverence by a flash of pure white as a brilliant albino squirrel scampered up a tree a few feet away. It stopped on the trunk, level with my head and stared at me, its tiny body twitching as it tried to decide if I was truly a threat. It was gorgeous and I could only stand there, as still as possible, and pray that it would stay with me for a few more moments. As we watched each other I began to speak softly, apologizing for disturbing its foraging, promising that I meant no harm, thanking it for blessing me with its presence. It soon decided there were more important things to be done and leapt high into the branches of the tree, throwing a scolding chirp over its shoulder as it went. I laughed and continued on my walk.

Two blocks later I almost stumbled over another squirrel as it dashed out from a nearby shrub and crossed the sidewalk in front of me. Again, I stopped and stared. This one was a beautiful deep black with bright, dark eyes that watched me warily from the edge of the grass. After a few seconds it shot across the street and out of sight. I stood there and shook my head, smiling softly at my encounter with the yin and yang of the Universe. By slowing down with intentional presence and respect, I had been given an opportunity to find balance. I felt solid, grounded firmly in my place within the miracle of existence; and my spirit soared, singing in praise and gratitude for the beauty of this Earth.

Resurrection

I have, at times in my life, struggled with depression. During those times I always turn to music – both creating it and listening to it. There are songs that have held me as I've wept. Songs that have renewed hope. Songs that have helped me find life again.

Many years ago, during a particularly rough time, I was living in a place where I didn't have a piano – and that is never a good thing. Fortunately, a friend of mine was able to somehow get me a key to a Catholic Church she attended – and they had a baby grand piano I could play.

So I would go, late at night, slip in through the shadows, into the silent sanctuary.

I would leave the lights off and remove my shoes. Light a few candles in prayer.

And then sit down and pour my heart out, playing whatever came, whatever needed to be said.

Whatever needed to be heard.

There I would sit, barefoot in the dark, weeping as I found life again through music in that still, sacred space - practicing resurrection with every note I played.

Multitudes

So, a strange thing happened the other day. I was sitting in our sunroom on a beautiful, crisp, early spring day. It was late afternoon and the sun was just hovering over the trees before it began its evening descent. There were just a few clouds in the sky and the bright blue contrasted sharply with the deep green of the pines and firs, as they all basked in the rays of the setting sun. Suddenly, a shout came from somewhere in the house behind me, "It's snowing!" And I looked out to see tiny crystals drifting down, dancing in the breeze, glittering in the sunlight. I looked again to the clear sky. I looked again to the full sun. And I marveled that even still there was snow. I jumped up, slid open a glass door, and stepped outside, spreading my arms and tilting my head back to catch a few flakes – just like I had done as a child, laughing in delight as I twirled my body around, joining the snow dance in the light of the sun.

Let me remind you that this is a world of both/and, not either/or.

You live in a world that is both slowly dying,
And that is blooming back to life in verdant beauty.

You live in a world in which the tree is both itself and the forest,
The water is both the droplet and the ocean,
A world of both sunshine and snow,
Where the sun sets each night, leaving us to dwell in darkness,
And that same sun rises every single morning.
No matter what, the sun rises.

This planet, your home, needs you to be full of contradictions.
Needs you to be both a fierce activist and a tender healer,

Full of both the bright warmth of compassion
And the crystal sharpness of conviction.
Our Mother Earth needs you to be both sunshine and snow.

You are made of rain.
You are made of ocean waves and tidal pools,
of moonlight and stardust,
the language of birds and the songs of the wind.
You are desert and mountain,
canyon, island, jungle, plains.

You are no more than a drop of water,
A grain of sand,
A single leaf being carried down the stream of life.

And, as Whitman says, you "contain multitudes."

The dust of dinosaurs dwells within your skin,
The breath of every bird that has ever sung its song to the morning
sun moves through your lungs,
The water that held the very beginnings of life as they birthed
themselves into being runs through your blood;
As plates shifted, as land moved, as oceans parted,
and as the blistering core of this earth erupted,
as sheets of ice continents-wide crawled their way across the land,
in that way the fire and ice of creation, of conviction, of
commitment
thunders within you still.

You are sunshine,
burning with hope,
encouraging life,
bringing to light beauty
and brokenness.

You are snow,
a flake and a flurry;
you are rain,
a drop and a deluge,
falling on every land,
on every tree,
on every tongue.
Nourishing and washing clean.

You are the tree
and we are the forest.

CLOSING WORDS

> Our actions shape the environment and the environment shapes our overall well-being. The future is open-ended and we have a role in shaping the future, for good or ill.
>
> — BRUCE EPPERLY, *PROCESS THEOLOGY AND MYSTICISM*

In this way you, in soulful collaboration with the universe, are discovering, creating, growing, evolving your own personal theology. The act of you noticing, seeing, celebrating, discovering, encouraging the sacred in the world around you <u>makes</u> it sacred, it becomes holy - a part of your understanding of and relationship with the Divine. Which in turn <u>changes you</u> and affects who and how you are in the world.

In her groundbreaking science fiction work *The Parable of the Sower*, Octavia Butler created the Earthseed religion. One of the tenets of that (process theology inspired) faith is this:

All that you touch you change.
All that you change changes you.

She also wrote:

Belief
Initiates and guides action—
Or it does nothing.

I once heard leadership trainer J. Tyson Casey speak about what he called "sustainable leadership." He says life is a series of surprises and as we encounter each surprise we must ask ourselves, "What can I do in this moment that will cultivate the conditions for life?"

How can we create change that enables the capacity *for all* to thrive?

Visionary adrienne maree brown says that we must learn to listen, without assumptions or defenses, with humility and selflessness and patience and rhythm, that we must practice generosity and vulnerability. She says that "our work has to be nuanced and steadfast. And more than anything, that we need each other."

Go Deep, Again and Again

Sometimes we are the piece of glass being tumbled and thrown around. Sometimes we are the waves, the tides, the salty sea, shaping and transforming the world around us, changing all that comes within our reach.

Wade in again and again - go deeper each time. Experiment and adapt. You cannot even begin to imagine what you will discover.

Take a breath, center yourself, and look with fresh eyes - the tide that returns each day is never composed of the same water; each time the sun rises, a new dance of atoms and light showers down upon us; each morning when you arise, each encounter you have, with every single breath you take there is possibility and opportunity for transformative creativity.

Dive deep and see what you find.

A Deep Dive

We've taken a deep dive,
a great leap of faith.
Here in the waters of the unknown,
time slows,
sounds are muted,
the light changes,
images waver,
and our bodies move in different ways,
weightless and heavy,
sinking yet buoyant.

If we let go –
let go! –
trust in the water,
this water,
to hold us,
support us,
to keep us afloat
and offer a different perspective.

For even at the depth of the deepest lake,
even at rock bottom,
even when we feel like we're drowning,
the smallest speck of light
can shine through,
leading us back to the surface,

a surface alive with possibility,
teeming with life,
gleaming in the sunlight
of this world we are creating together.

Take a deep breath,
take my hand,
let go and leap with me again
Over and over into the ever-changing sea.
Let's see where the water takes us this time.

Acknowledgments

In memory of Rob and Janne Eller-Isaacs, who not only mentored me into ministry but encouraged my search for, and expression of, my deepest truth. It was their passion and commitment to my journey that built much of this book.

To all the congregants, colleagues, and classmates who both inspired and critiqued many of these essays along the way. My writing wouldn't exist without you.

For my family, all the many of you, who provided the context and grounding from which all else flows – it is your support through the entirety of my life that gives me hope, especially when I could not have imagined how you would continue to love me. Most importantly, great gratitude to my mom, who first and foremost sees me as a daughter to be proud of, regardless of the differences in our lives; in honor of my dad, the traveler who packed us up every summer and shared the world with us; and in memory of my grandma Rose, the purest spiritual guide I've ever met – thank you for teaching me how to embody faith, how to preach without words, and how to love whole-heartedly.

To Angela and Tehom Center Publishing for encouraging and embracing me into this project, and for all the work you do of giving voice to those so often unheard.

And finally, to Diana, the sunshine and warmth of my life, my own private book editor and cheerleader, thank you for being my partner in all our adventures. Truly, this book would never have been printed if not for your gentle nudges to get it done.

Sources and Resources

Books

brown, adrienne maree. *Emergent Strategy: Shaping Change, Changing Worlds*. AK Press, 2017.

Butler, Octavia E. *Parable of the Sower*. Four Walls Eight Windows, 1993.

—. *Parable of the Talents*. Seven Stories Press, 1998.

Chodron, Pema. *The Places that Scare You*. Shambhala Library, 2005.

de Gaulle, Charles. *The Edge of the Sword*. Faber and Faber, 1960.

Duffy, Kathleen. *Teilhard's Mysticism: Seeing the Inner Face of Evolution*. Orbis Books, 2014.

Eliot, T. S. *Four Quartets: A Poem*. Faber & Faber, 1944.

Emerson. "Circles". *Essays and Lectures*. Library of America, 1983,

Epperly, Bruce G. *Process Theology: Embracing Adventure with God*. Energion Publications, 2014.

—. *Process Theology and Mysticism*. Energion Publications, 2024.

Fox, Matthew. *Creation Spirituality: Liberating Gifts for the Peoples of the Earth*. Harper Collins, 1991.

Lewis, C.S. *The Weight of Glory*. Macmillan, 1945.

McColman, Carl. *The Big Book of Christian Mysticism: The Essential Guide to Contemplative Spirituality*. Broadleaf Books, 2021.

McGinn, Bernard. *The Presence of God* book series. Crossroad Publishing, 2004-2021.

Nin, Anaïs. "Abstraction". *The Novel of the Future*. Third Printing. Collier Books: A Division of Macmillan Publishing Company, New York, 1976.

Nouwen, Henri. *Reaching Out: The Three Movements of Spiritual Life*. Doubleday & Company, 1975.

Phillips, Jan. *The Art of Original Thinking: The Making of a Thought Leader*. 9th Element Press, 2006.

—. *Divining the Body: Reclaim the Holiness of Your Physical Self*. SkyLight Paths, 2005.

Shklovsky, Viktor. "Art as Technique." *Literary Theory: An Anthology*. Ed. Julie Rivkin and Michael Ryan. Malden: Blackwell Publishing Ltd, 1998.

Taggart, John. *Is Music: New and Selected Poems*. Copper Canyon Press, 2010.

Thoreau, Henry David. "Walden". *Henry David Thoreau*. Library of America, 1985.

Whitman, Walt. "Song of Myself". *Whitman: Poetry and Prose*. Library of America, 1982.

Williamson, Marianne. *Illuminata: A Return to Prayer*. Random House, 1994.

Online Articles

Hanh, Thich Nhat. "This Moment is Perfect." *Lion's Roar Magazine*. https://www.lionsroar.com/the-moment-is-perfect/. Accessed November 8, 2024.

McDaniel, Jay. "Twenty Key Ideas in the Process Worldview." *Open Horizons.* https://www.openhorizons.org/twenty-key-ideas-in-process-thinking.html. Accessed November 8, 2024.

Weldon, Amy. "The Spinning Self: On Pottery and the Rest of My Life." *Bloom.* https://bloomsite.wordpress.com/2014/12/19/the-spinning-self-on-pottery-and-the-rest-of-my-life/. Accessed November 8, 2024.

Websites

The Center for Action and Contemplation: www.cac.org

The Earthseed Religion: www.godischange.org

Open Horizons: www.openhorizons.org

www.ingramcontent.com/pod-product-compliance
Lightning Source LLC
Chambersburg PA
CBHW061712120626

46550CB00003B/1192